SHANGRI-LA

[ALONG THE TEA ROAD TO LHASA]

PHOTOGRAPHS AND TEXT BY
MICHAEL YAMASHITA

TEXT EDITOR
ELIZABETH BIBB

PROJECT EDITOR
VALERIA MANFERTO DE FABIANIS

EDITORIAL ASSISTANT
LAURA ACCOMAZZO

GRAPHIC DESIGN
PAOLA PIACCO

Contents

FOREWORD: IN SEARCH OF PARADISE	PAGE 12
INTRODUCTION: SHANGRI-LA AND BEYOND	PAGE 20
CHAPTER 1: ALL THE TEA IN CHINA	PAGE 30
CHAPTER 2: MYSTIC MOUNTAINS AND MONASTERIES	PAGE 60
CHAPTER 3: CULTURAL HEART AND SOUL	PAGE 98
CHAPTER 4: NOMADS LAND	PAGE 160
CHAPTER 5: ON THE ROAD TO LHASA AND THE TOP OF THE WORLD	PAGE 206
CHAPTER 6: ELUSIVE SHANGRI-LA	PAGE 246
BIOGRAPHIES, BIBLIOGRAPHY AND ACKNOWLEDGMENTS	PAGE 270

In Search of Paradise

It all started in Jiuzhaigou, China's most popular—and most remote—national park. Located in northern Sichuan province, this is a place where crystal-clear waters cascade from glacial peaks into a progression of emerald lakes, ponds, streams and rivulets, punctuated by blue-green waterfalls and luxurious vegetation. According to legend, the park's 118 crystalline lakes were formed after a Tibetan god gave a mirror polished by the clouds and the wind to a goddess, who then dropped it, scattering its shards over what is now Jiuzhaigou. Discovered by loggers in the 1960s, this enchanted place, whose name means The Valley of Nine Villages, is known by few Chinese and even fewer foreigners. Ninety percent of its 20,000 daily visitors are Chinese. My Chinese photographer friends all name Jiuzhaigou as the most photogenic place in China.

It was in Jiuzhaigou that I first heard of the ancient trade route, the Chamagudao, or Tea Horse Road, which began over 2500 years ago when Chinese merchants started trading tea to Tibetans in exchange for horses, which China needed to defend against the constant threat of mounted Mongol invasions. It soon became a conduit not just for tea and horses, but also for cultural exchange. Remote ethnic groups traded goods and customs along a patchwork of mountain trails that led to some of the farthest reaches of the Tibetan plateau. Part of this network of roads still winds through Jiuzhaigou.

Awed by this Chinese fairyland and intrigued by stories about the Chamagudao, I proposed a story on Jiuzhaigou to my editors at *National Geographic* magazine, where I have worked for the past 32 years. For four blissful weeks, spread over three seasons, I marveled at the unbelievably over-the-top—almost to the point of garish—vibrant colors around me. So vibrant were they that I was a little worried that readers of the magazine would think I had over Photoshopped the files on this one. Jiuzhaigou became, and still remains, my personal vision of paradise, a photographer's Shangri-La in every sense of the word. The photographs I made there whetted my appetite for more discoveries along the fabled trade route. After completing my story on Jiuzhaigou (which was published by *National Geographic Magazine* in March 2009), I was ready to follow the Chamagudao further, on what would become a two-year search (and another magazine story) for other hidden Shangri-Las.

As I often say in my workshops and lectures around the world, it is a photographer's job, as well as his biggest challenge, to photograph a subject in a way that is different from whatever has been done before. Before beginning any assignment, I do my research, reading every article and trying to find every picture that's ever been shot on my subject, to become the expert on every aspect of the story I'm about to begin. In the case of the Tea Horse Road, though, there was surprisingly little research material

to study. I found a few books translated from Chinese, none with photography, and a number of websites offering off-the-beaten path tours in and around Greater Tibet—Yunnan Sichuan, and Qinghai provinces—and the Tibet Autonomous Region (TAR).

Perhaps the size and scope of the subject—three main routes crisscrossing the mountains, lakes and rivers of the Tibetan Plateau—put it logistically out of the reach of most magazine and book publishers. Also, its web of mountain passes, highways and trails branching out in all directions over varied terrain and cultures made finding a central focus, a narrative "hook," challenging. But rather than discourage me, the complexity of the subject became my most motivating factor in embarking on a story about the Chamagudao. This was exactly my kind of assignment—a new story on a subject all but unknown outside of China, big and complex enough to warrant at least a year's coverage for National Geographic.

By the early spring of 2008, just a few months before the Beijing Olympics, I was planning to start my coverage with the first picking of the tea harvest in Yaan, in Sichuan province, where the northern branch of the Chamagudao began. China couldn't have been in a better mood, with everyone busy with final preparations for the country's big coming-out party of the new millennium.

Then, on March 15, the anniversary of the 1959 Tibetan uprising against the armed takeover by the Chinese, riots erupted in Lhasa and in Kham, west of Chengdu. In response, the Chinese government closed all roads leading to Tibet to foreigners. So for most of 2008, I spent my time in China shooting—and tasting—a lot of tea, waiting for permits to allow me enter the Tibetan region and begin my travels along the Chamagudao.

Tea is a whole subject unto itself, and there's no better place than China to experience it, since all tea originated there. That's a bold statement considering how many different types of tea there are today, not to mention the ever-expanding number of places tea is now grown. But it's generally believed that the birthplace of tea drinking is in the far southern tropical regions of Yunnan province. The area's elevation, climate and rainfall make it perfect for tea cultivation. I first visited this region in the early 1990s, working on a National Geographic story tracing the Mekong River from its source on the Tibetan Plateau in Qinghai province to its mouth in Vietnam. Passing through the town of Puer, which is in the Xishuangbanna region of Yunnan, I photographed the harvesting and processing of one of China's most expensive teas. I took hundreds of frames, shooting the various stages of tea production, from sorting and drying to grading and packing, but only one photograph from that shoot—of a mother and daughter covered by a plastic sheet, picking tea leaves in the rain—was published in the magazine. So I welcomed that chance to revisit the subject. Tea, after all, was half of what made the Chamagudao what it was—the Tea Horse Road.

- 2-3 Buddhist nuns at Shusong Nunnery in Benzilan, study ancient texts.
- 4-5 Tibetan girls are decked in festival finery, turquoise, coral and silver.
- 6-7 Prayer flags fly over the turquoise waters of the sacred Lhamo Latso Lake.
- 8-9 Huge trucks are mere pin-dots along the 16,404 ft (5000 m) Trola Pass east of Dege.
- 10-11 Sumzanling Monastery presides over the hillside of Shangri-la (once known as Zhongdian), in Yunnan province and may have been the inspiration for the lamasery in Lost Horizon.
- 12-13 The author/photographer in Tibet.
- 14-15 Winter's last blast at Five Color Lake in Jiuzhaigou National Park.

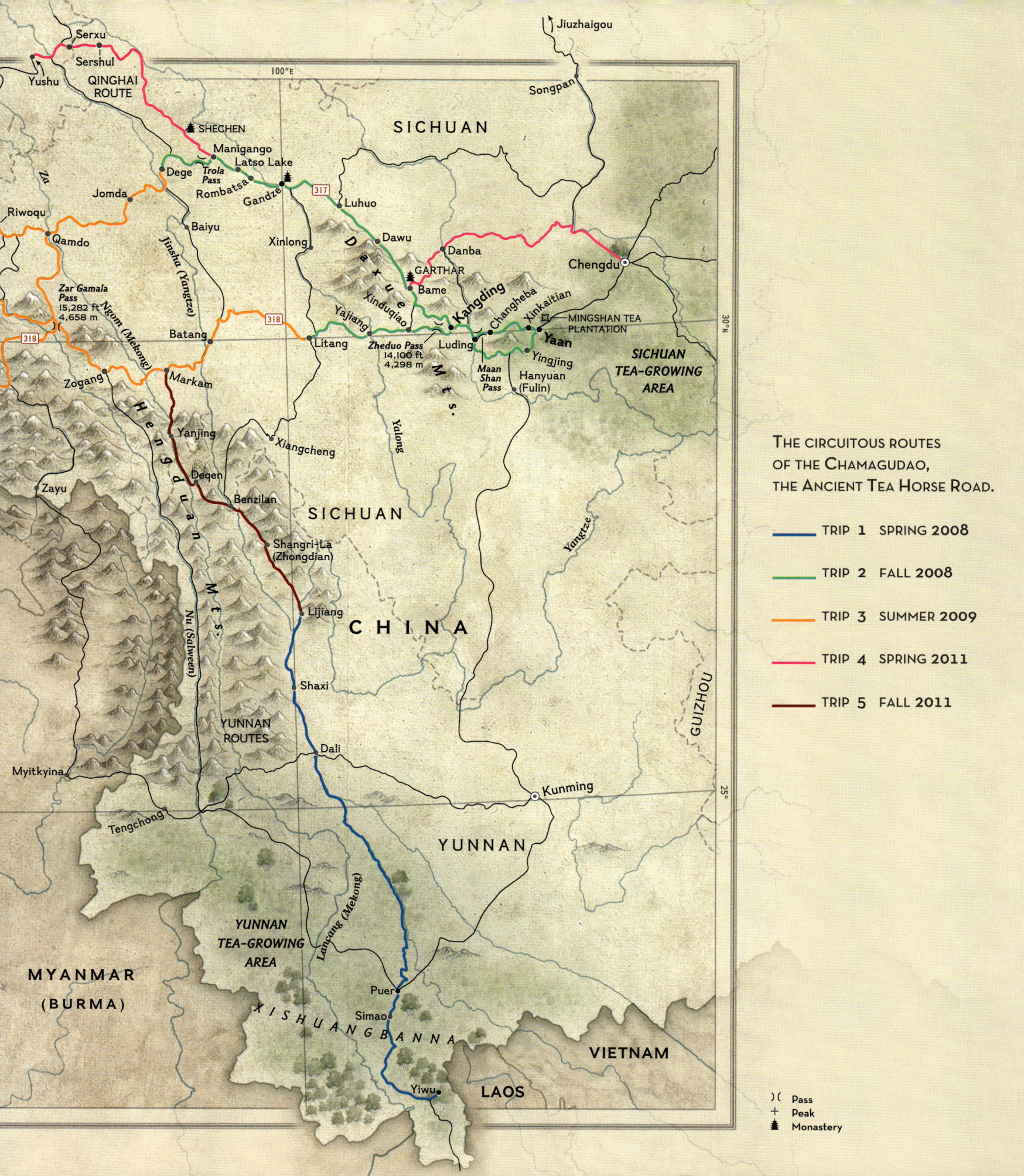

Shangri-La and Beyond

by ELIZABETH BIBB

Shangri-La was lovely then, touched with the mystery that lies at the core of all loveliness.
-Lost Horizon by James Hilton

When conjuring images of Shangri-La, the fictitious paradise on earth conceived by James Hilton in his 1933 novel, mystery is the operative term. Despite the fact that Hilton's magical land where men and women lived in harmony and never aged was purely fiction, the mystery he evoked has continued to lead fans of the book to speculate as to Hilton's inspiration for the hidden kingdom of Shangri-La. Some of the likeliest candidates are high in the Himalayan Mountains. With its hundreds of lamaseries hovering amid mist-shrouded peaks, windswept plains and pastoral valleys, immersed in mystery and contradictions, Tibet and western China certainly look the part. The area's beauty and remoteness, the complex rituals of its unique form of Buddhism, the ruggedness of its people who live at dizzying altitudes all contribute to the mystery. It seems a land apart from time, just as Hilton described his Shangri-La.

But as remote as the Tibetan Plateau is, the notion that Tibet has always been removed from contact with the outside world is challenged by the fact that since at least the seventh century, and perhaps long before, cultural exchange between Tibet and its neighbors has been ongoing. Among the conduits for this contact was a trade founded in mystery and legend, but which grew into a lucrative and mutually beneficial commercial and cultural exchange.

The roots of this exchange lie in *Camellia sinensis*—the species from which all tea leaves are plucked—from the tea forests of Yunnan to the tea plantations of Sichuan in Western China. China is believed to be the birthplace of tea. Growing wild in the mountains of Yunnan, in the semi-tropical southwest of China, it was discovered first to have medicinal properties, and later, to be a nutritious and savory drink. Tea's exact origins have been lost in legend; the most frequently cited being the story of the Chinese emperor who was pleasantly surprised when a leaf from a tea tree fell into his cup of boiling water, producing a delicious and healthful brew. That emperor is believed to have been Shen Nong, who is attributed with writing the Bencao, the Chinese Book of Medicine.

Tea soon became prized as a gift of tribute among nobles and as a way to endure long hours of meditation among Buddhist monks. Tea became more than a commodity; it was even used as a form of currency.

Exactly how tea found its way to remote Tibet, where tea cultivation was not possible, is lost in ancient folklore and legend. Often cited is the story of Wen Cheng, the Chinese princess who was promised in marriage to the Tibetan king, Songtsen Gampo. Among the many gifts and belongings she brought from China, tea was one of the most prized, along with a statue of the Shakyamuni Buddha.

However tea came to Tibet, it nevertheless became even more of a staple there than it was in China. Because of the Tibetan plateau's harsh climate and altitude, agriculture is severely limited. The indigenous diet is almost entirely protein and fat, with almost no vegetable matter to speak of. Tea, aside from being tasty and warming, provided much needed nutrients to the Tibetans. Tea, to a Tibetan, is as much a food as a drink. Mixed with yak butter or *tsampa*, a dough made with barley flour, tea was a way to extend a limited number of food choices. The fact that it also contains caffeine made it not only useful for staying alert during Buddhist meditation, but also addictive.

And once tea-drinking took hold, first among the nobles and monks of Tibet and later among nomads and farmers, the Chinese realized that the tea trade could be the answer to the ever-present problem of protecting its frontiers from invasion from the fierce nomadic tribes, including the Mongols to the north. China had something Tibet wanted, and Tibet, in turn, had something China needed—horses. During the Song Dynasty (960-1279), grazing land for horses was limited, and China was blocked to the north and east by the threat of invasion, so they turned to the Tibetans to supply sturdy and sure-footed horses that could withstand Himalayan weather and topography and help China's armies defend its borders.

This exchange of tea for horses grew into the development of the Chamagudao, a 1900-mile-long (3000 kilometer) network of trails and mountain passes along which caravans of horses and groups of porters and muleteers traveled between China and Tibet. It began during the Song Dynasty, and continued through the 20th century. Often referred to, incorrectly, as the southern Silk Road, the Chamagudao was just as important for commerce and cultural exchange.

By the middle of the Song Dynasty, as many as 25,000 horses a year crossed the mountains from Tibet into China. For much of the second half of the 11th century, up to 6.5 million pounds of tea per year traveled 900 miles (1450 km) from southwest Sichuan to Tibet. And by 1074, the Sichuan Tea Horse Administration was instituted, to promote, regulate and tax the trade.

There were two main routes of the Chamagudao: a northerly one, which ran from Yaan in Sichuan province through Gandze and Dege, as well as a more southerly system. But eventually all roads led to Lhasa, the heart and soul of Tibet, where traders, pilgrims and lamas all mingled, prayed, drank tea and conducted business.

Despite the assistance of Tibetan horses, the Mongols eventually conquered the Song, but the tea-horse trade continued through the Ming (1368-1644) and Qing (1644-1911) Dynasties. By the Qing Dynasty, 15.6 million pounds of tea went to Tibet each year, representing 90 percent of the Sichuan harvest.

One, the best tea from China,
Two, the pure dre *butter of Tibet,*
Three, the white salt from the northern plains, All three from different places,
All meeting in the copper pot.
Yet, how the tea is brewed is up to you, O tea maker.
(JAMYANG NORBU, WARRIORS OF TIBET, P. 15)

The tea favored by Tibetans was different from that most prized by the Chinese, due in part to a quest for a drink that would provide missing nutrients to their diets and would also be compatible with their staple diet of yak butter and meat, and barley. Tea bound for the Tibetan trade was known as border or brick tea (for the way in which it was pressed and packed for transport.) It was cultivated in Sichuan province, but tea from Yunnan, where tea trees grow wild and tall, was also exported.

Comprised not only of tea leaves, but also twigs and stems, brick tea was steamed or roasted, pressed into rectangular "bricks" and aged. This form of processing made it durable and portable for long treks across the mountains. Tea bricks were packed into long, narrow bamboo tubes (*bao*) for transport and loaded onto the backs of porters or mules. And because porters were paid by the pound, they tried to carry as many *bao* as possible. The strongest could tote up to 15 or more *bao* (the equivalent of 400 pounds or 180 kilograms).

There is a life-sized statue standing 20 minutes outside Yaan, commemorating these men who embarked on what amounted to death-defying ordeals across mountains to transport tea to Tibet. It is one of the few actual reminders of what these men endured. Only a handful of men are left to describe their hair-raising adventures. Their caravans of tea and horses battled fierce weather and breath-taking altitudes, but also the unseen dangers of the road—including robbers and bandits, jagged cliffs and narrow paths high above steep gorges, along which one wrong step could mean certain death. Those who survived had stories to tell about the mystic lands and mountains through which they traveled.

As the demand for tea and horses grew, monasteries, which were the spiritual and cultural heart of Tibet, became major trading centers. Many sponsored huge caravans, with monks being guaranteed safe progress along the route. This melding of religion and commerce resulted in monasteries growing rich in the process. Through the ages, the only thing more important than tea to Tibetans has been Buddhism, and it was largely through the tea trade and its many offshoots that the monasteries gained power and wealth. This mixing of the commercial and the spiritual can still be seen today, as pilgrims ply the paths of the Tea-Horse network, circumambulating holy mountains and temples.

Though the demand for horses diminished, trade between Tibet and China evolved, with brick tea being used as a form of currency up until the mid-20th century. Highways have replaced the complex network of passes and paths that led caravans back and forth over the mountains. And a different Tibetan commodity craved by China has replaced horses in the trade—the *yartsa gombu*. With the discovery of the amazing health benefits of this strange parasitic mushroom formed by consuming its host caterpillar, tent-dwelling nomads are becoming wealthy. But, tea remains a major import. Tibetans drink more tea than any other people on earth, and they depend on it for more than just libation. It is a sort of social cement, linking families, communities, and strangers, as well as integral element in the ritual and traditions of Tibetan Buddhism.

Just as Shangri-La is said to be an idea, not a place, the winding Tea Horse Road, too, is an idea. More than the once highly traveled trade route or its cobble-stoned remnants today, the Chamagudao opened the eyes of the world to the mysteries of Tibet and brought the outside world into Tibet. Passing through some of the most sublime, yet treacherous landscapes in the world, this route will always mean more than mere commerce. This is the route that enticed travelers with earthly riches, but for those who were willing to see them, it also held more ethereal treasures. The Chamagudao is like the mystical "sky road" that leads from *Shambhala* (the Sanskrit term for the hidden utopia Hilton imagined). Embodying the contradictions one sees even today in this region of the earth, where the worldly coexists with the spiritual in a constant dance, a journey along the Chamagudao leads those who travel it on their own search for Shangri-La.

- 16-17 Pearl Shoals Falls, with a drop height of 69 ft (21 m), cascades into a shawl of pearls draped across a hillside.
- 24-25 Tibetan Gedong Mask Dancing: monks perform this yearly ritual dancing in occasion of the Gedong Festival.
- 26-27 A steaming cauldron of yak butter tea will serve 800 monks at Shechen Monastery.
- 28-29 The faithful light yak butter lamps in honor of a Living Buddha during an 18-day festival of prayers in Bame.

All the Tea in China

chapter 1

All the Tea in China

Chapter One

Xishuangbanna is considered the birthplace of tea; legend has it that here, in 2737 BC, Emperor Shen Nong, a revered scholar and herbalist, discovered the pleasures of tea drinking when a tea leaf floated into his cup of boiling water. That's why when I arrived there, I headed for Nan Luo Shan, one of the six famous mountains of the region where the best teas are said to grow. Nan Luo Shan is known for its indigenous forests of wild tea trees, and I was looking for one in particular, reputed to be over 1200 years old. Called the "King of Tea Trees" by the locals, it turned out to be less than impressive. It was only 30 ft (9 m) high, past its prime and no longer harvested. It looked like an old apple tree enshrined behind a fence. Underwhelmed, I went in search of a better subject. I found one, though younger (800 years old) and shorter (only 20 ft [6 m] high), but with a cluster of Dai minority women perching precariously in its highest branches picking new spring leaves.

Tea picking is considered an ideal job for women, as they are lighter and reputedly have better climbing skills than men. The sight of women clad in brightly-colored costumes, holding bamboo baskets full of tea aloft in an ancient tree is a far cry from the waves of perfectly sculpted tea hedges undulating across terraced hills that we usually associate with tea cultivation. But without trimming, those manicured tea bushes would eventually grow into trees just like the ones I was shooting.

At the time, I was not a regular tea drinker, even though in China, where I most frequently work, the ubiquitous cup is a part of almost every social gathering. Given the choice, though, I preferred a black espresso to jolt me awake for most morning shoots. And until now, I had always thought that Japan's ritualized tea ceremony, with its roots in Zen Buddhism and elaborate preparation of powdered *macha*, represented the highest level of tea culture. On this assignment, though, I discovered that the Chinese scoff at the thought of drinking tea ground into a fine powder. I learned this and more about the intricacies of China's national drink from my Dai host and the owner of the plantation where I was shooting, Yan Yi Di.

We sat out on the veranda of his house, built on stilts, sipping green tea from a glass with newly picked, dried and rolled tea leaves, regarded as the best crop of the year. I watched, fascinated, as the leaves bobbed up and down in the hot water, slowly unfurling to reveal their full shape. Yan then proceeded to introduce me to the *gong fu* tea ceremony of Puer tea. While most Westerners usually associate *gong fu* or *kung fu*, with Chinese martial arts, the term actually refers to any skill that is achieved after much training and effort. It was clear that Yan was a master.

Yan began by pouring hot water over a small clay teapot and two tiny one-shot porcelain tea cups several times to warm them up. Next he added a small pinch of tea cut from a disc-shaped cake of pressed tea to the pot and poured more water over it to clean the leaves. He then discarded the water. I had to wait for a few more pours and discards until Yan offered me my first taste of the dark amber liquid. This was followed by three or four more pours and tastes of the original brew, then followed by pours and tastes of several other varieties of leaves (so many I lost count). Each cupful was different, depending on the age and type of tree and leaf. The idea is to prolong and enhance the enjoyment of the tea through multiple infusions and scents, since in gong fu, all the senses should be engaged. After countless tastes of tea, my senses were fully activated, and my caffeine buzz kept me wide-eyed and awake well into the night, but it was the beginning of a new taste and appreciation for tea… I was hooked.

Xishuangbanna may be the birthplace of tea, but Yaan in Sichuan province is where the first tea bush was planted and cultivated over 3000 years ago. It was also the starting point for the second main artery of the Chamagudao, now known as the Sichuan-Tibet Highway Route 317.

Though tea was likely introduced to Tibet through Buddhism, as a caffeinated aid for long hours of meditation, it served another crucial purpose: nutrition. The harsh climate and rugged terrain of Tibet made agriculture difficult and tea cultivation impossible. As a result, the Tibetan diet still consists primarily of protein and fats—meats and milk, cheese and butter from yaks. Tea became indispensible as a vegetable substitute due to its vitamin and mineral content. Stronger tasting than the more expensive Puer tea from Yunnan, Yaan "brick" tea is said to be more compatible with the bitterness of yak butter, into which it is commonly mixed.

With this growing Tibetan dependence on tea, the Chinese realized that they could barter for prized Tibetan horses. By 1074, during the Song Empire, the Tea and Horse Office was established in Yaan to oversee this trade. And though China now has little use for Tibetan horses, Tibetans remain the biggest tea drinkers in the world, consuming 30 to 40 cups a day and up to 22 pounds (10 kg) of leaves a year. The tea grown in Yaan still accounts for 90 percent of the tea exported to Tibet.

In Yaan's Ming Shan County, they call their plantations tea gardens, and for good reason. They are as carefully planned and sculpted as a Japanese garden with pavilions and walkways to show off its most photogenic angles. Visitors come for walking tours, as much for the scenery as for the famous tea. The town is also home to the only Tibetan-owned and -operated tea factory, where tea is packaged according to a traditional process going back 1000 years. At the Namse Tibetan Tea Factory, rough-cut tea leaves, along with twigs and stems, are roasted and then rammed while still hot into woven oblong bamboo baskets. Known as "brick" tea because of its shape, tea from Yaan was transported along the Chamagudao, all the way to Lhasa and beyond, wherever Tibetans and Tibetan culture could be found.

• **34-35** Terraces of tea unfold along the hillside of the largest tea plantation in Xishuangbanna, Yunnan province, the number one producer of prized Puer tea.

● **36-37** Pickers dot the waves of cultivated tea at one of the three largest plantations in Yaan, Sichuan province, where the northern route of the Tea Horse Road starts.

● **38-39** Tea trees grow tall and wild in Yunnan province. Here a fearless picker balances in the branches of a 1000-year-old specimen. The rule of thumb is: the taller the tree, the higher the price of the leaves.

● **40-41** The view from Songtsam Lodge in Tacheng, overlooks terraced rice paddies. The local farming community of Tibetans, Lisu, and Naxi Minorities have been working this valley for centuries, thanks to it's mild climate and fertile soil.

• **42-43** The Bai town of Shaxi in Yunnan province is one of the most intact caravan towns on the Chamagudao, where a former tea administration building and many tea shops can be found.

• **43** In the village of Yiwu, in Yunnan province, children play on remnants of the original southern Tea Horse Road, which began near here.

• **44-45** A man brings his sow and her family to market along the same road through Shaxi that was traveled by the tea and horse traders of centuries ago.

• **46-47** Time for play: elders in Shaxi's town square are intent upon their board games and *mah jong* tiles.

● 48-49 Time for work: Husband and wife are equally intent on binding bundles of mung beans in the living room of their home near Dali, an important stop along the Tea Horse Road.

● **50-51** Farmers thrash their crop of mung beans outside the weathered walls of Dali. The Tea Horse Road once ran through this picturesque high mountain village, which has remained unchanged for a thousand years.

● **52-53** In Yiwu, tea leaves dry in the sun outside the oldest tea factory in Yunnan. This earthy-tasting black tea known as Puer originated in this area of southwestern China.

● **54-55 AND 55** PUER TEA IS STEAMED AND PRESSED INTO FLAT CAKES AS IT HAS BEEN FOR HUNDREDS OF YEARS. HERE AT YIWU'S BAO PU SHAN TEA FACTORY, SEVEN GENERATIONS HAVE PRODUCED THE HIGHEST QUALITY TEA.

• **56** Packing Puer tea for shipment in Menghai – seven tea cakes are fitted into bamboo-shoot husk wrappers. Horses and mules once would each carry four baskets loaded with six of these packages.

• **56-57** Workers wrap cakes of Puer tea in paper at the Riu Xiang Tea Factory in Menghai, Yunnan.

● 58-59 A TEA MASTER PERFORMS AN ELABORATE GONG FU TEA CEREMONY AT A RETAIL SHOP IN PUER.

chapter 2
Mystic Mountains and Monasteries

Mystic Mountains and Monasteries
Chapter Two

The Sichuan-Tibet Highway (Route 317) runs roughly 1400 mi (2400 km) from Yaan to Lhasa, over what the *Lonely Planet Guide* describes as "one of the world's highest, roughest, most dangerous and most beautiful roads." It wasn't until late fall 2008 that I got the opportunity to travel this section of the Chamagudao. Because of unrest in the Greater Tibetan regions, including the border areas of the Gansu, Sichuan, Qinghai and Yunnan provinces, access had been blocked to outsiders since March 2008. But Kham, the area along Tibet's eastern edge that straddles Sichuan, had been relatively quiet and without demonstrations, so by November, China began allowing foreigners to visit there again. I jumped at the chance.

Route 317 traverses some 28 mountain passes over 9800 ft (3000 m) high. As we were about to cross the over 14,000 ft (4200 m) Zheduo Pass, the gateway to the Tibetan Plateau, I was glad to have the services of an ace driver, Huka. His small frame and boyish features hide a physical toughness and intense ability to concentrate that allows him to drive for hours on end without falling asleep. He is a master behind the wheel of his 1997 Land Cruiser, the hands-down undisputed car of choice for tackling the harsh conditions for which Routes 317 is infamous. Huka constantly sips tea from a flask, replenishing with hot water at every stop and is the only one I'd say who works longer days than a photographer, from warming up the car for our departure before sunrise to unpacking at our nightly accommodations. Safety is Huka's obsession, since the hazards of the Tea Horse Road are many. From blind curves to hair-raising hairpins, roads of ice to seas of mud, dense fog to deep snow, rogue truck drivers hogging the road to prostrating pilgrims oblivious to traffic—nothing fazes Huka.

As was to become our habit, we stopped the Land Cruiser at the top of Zheduo Pass and took a deep breath of the cold, clear, thin mountain air, acclimating to the high altitude. The steep mountain passes are the most dangerous for travelers on the Chamagudao, since at high altitudes, snow can come at anytime. It may be summer down below, but at over 13,000 ft (4000 m), the weather can change in minutes, suddenly calling for a quick switch from short-sleeved shirts and shorts to down jackets and Gore-Tex.

Given their hazards, all passes in Tibetan territory are festooned with prayer flags, and Zheduo, befitting its status as the first pass leading into the Tibetan Plateau, also had a Chinese-style pavilion built atop the mountain, completely decked out in fiercely fluttering flags 300 ft (100 m) above the road. These pieces of cloth known as dar cho in Tibetan are

the colors of the rainbow, printed with prayers or mantras as offerings to the gods, blessings for the mountains and to bring good luck to travelers who cross in often treacherous weather conditions. And since the wind blows everywhere, the prayers messages are communicated all over the country. The winds this day were especially strong. On our first day at high elevation we struggled to climb, hearts pounding, ten steps at a time, followed by a short rest, then another ten, and so on. Reaching the top we were rewarded with breathtaking views (no pun intended).

Low, slow-moving clouds filled the valley floor, swallowing the traffic along the more than 60 switchbacks below. Only white headlights or red brake lights occasionally punched through the fog, adding a modern focal point to the scene. The strong winds, frozen fingers and a rapidly beating heart made it difficult to get a sharp frame, as I struggled to control my breathing. I wished I had a tripod, but was not about to go back down to the cars and bring one up. Bracing myself against the sturdy poles of the pavilion I worked quickly and retreated down the mountain as the sun faded.

Weather along the Chamagudao may be unpredictable, but one thing you can always count on is that any travel in China will be plagued by construction delays. Traffic can be stopped anytime, for hours or even days, due to bad roads, broken down vehicles or the whim of a road boss who needs to blast a rock or build a bridge. That meant we averaged less than 20 mi (30 km) an hour most days. Such were the conditions en route to Bame, where we were to photograph a religious festival at a small roadside monastery presided over by a Living Buddha, Longdo Rinpoche.

Arriving a day late due to the road construction, I was struck by the large numbers of Han Chinese devotees who sat among the Tibetans and crimson-robed Buddhist monks of all ages, all in rapt attention as the Rinpoche spoke. Children, goats, and dogs roamed in and out between groups of worshippers. Even a rain shower did nothing to dislodge these pilgrims who, as if by magic, produced umbrellas to keep dry. The acrid smell of yak butter was pervasive, as a huge cauldron in the middle of the field bubbled with buttery oil to fuel thousands of votive lamps, which were lit inside a smoke-filled windowless room in honor of the Rinpoche. Volunteer Tibetan women prepared and carried thermoses of hot yak butter tea to the crowds.

Butter tea is the Tibetan national drink, but with its salty, oily and sometimes rancid flavor it is also an acquired taste. More like a broth than what most Westerners think of as tea, it is made by boiling black "brick" tea for hours, to which salt and yak butter are added and then churned into froth. High in calories, the tea provides warmth and energy needed to survive in Tibet's high altitudes. And it is impossible to visit a Tibetan home, tent, monastery or event without being invited to drink some. Once introductions have been made, the incredibly hospitable Tibetans rarely let you take leave without drinking at least three cups, never letting your cup go more than half empty.

After many years of polite imbibing, I have finally acquired the taste, though I prefer fresh yak butter—the less rancid the better. I drink it often, as the Tibetans do, for an energy boost and to take the edge off the cold temperatures outside. And as my story was about tea, I took advantage of every drinking situation to photograph as well as refresh. This event was no exception.

A little later, as if on cue, the rains stopped, the sun shone, and a perfect double rainbow formed over a field of *chorten* (stupas). It was hard not to be moved by the day's events as I tallied and captioned my photos and downloaded my flash cards that evening in a cozy room at a local guesthouse, which was painted in psychedelic Christmas reds and greens.

● **63** Zeduo Pass, the gateway to Tibet from western China, at 14,100 ft (4298 m) was once traversed by mule and horse caravans, but now trucks push on through the mist en route to Kanding.

● **65** Colorful stupas (*chorden*, in Tibet) in Bame, Sichuan province stand at attention, as if in awe of the fortuitous double rainbows arcing above during a sudden sun shower.

● **66-67** Prayer flags, placed by pilgrims to ensure safe travel, wave over Zheduo Pass, high above the mist-filled valley.

● **68-69** Bame's 18-day festival honoring a living Buddha, Longdo Rinpoche, draws devout pilgrims from all over Tibet to listen to the Rinpoche's addresses.

• **70-71** Danba, with its distinctive watchtowers in the distance, was voted the most beautiful village in China. It is also known for its traditional Tibetan architecture.

• **72-73** A family of farmers take a tea break before getting back to harvesting barley, which is mixed with yak butter tea to prepare *tsampa*, a staple of the Tibetan diet.

• **74-75** A tractor transports monks en route to Segyagu in Sichuan province.

• **76-77** Children peer from intricately decorated windows, framed by traditional Tibetan architecture that is fast disappearing.

● 78-79 AND 79 A LOADED TRACTOR ROLLS PAST A FORTRESS-LIKE HOME IN DANBA, KNOWN AS "THE KINGDOM OF WATCHTOWERS" AND "BEAUTY VALLEY."

● 80-81 Ci Zhu La Mu and her husband, Sun Nuo, entertain guests serving yak butter tea in their summer pasture home where they live with their yaks.

● 82-83 The remote monastery in Litang, said to be the highest on the planet, with an altitude of over 13,000 ft (4000 m) was founded in 1580 and is one of the largest in Kham.

● 84 Young monks spend most of their days studying Buddhist scripture both inside Garthar Monastery and *en plein air*.

● 85 A monk prepares a steaming pot of yak butter tea at Garthar Monastery.

● 86-87 Locals, who have been invited to Garthar Monastery during a festival, engage in the various stages of the highly ritualized practice of prostration called *chak tsal*, which means "to sweep clean."

• **88** A huge pile of *mani*, inscribed prayer stones, pave the way to the Segyagu meditation center, near Lhagong Monastery, whose monks are in the Yellow Hat sect.

• **88-89** The faithful perform the *kora*, circumambulating the temple, turning large prayer wheels as they go, to ensure good *karma*.

• **90-91** In Bame, locals help prepare yak butter lamps in preparation for an 18-day religious festival, honoring a Living Buddha, Longdo Rinpoche

● 92-93, 94-95 AND 96-97 DONGZHULIN MONASTERY, HIGH ATOP A RIDGE OVER THE YANGTZE. THIS 300 YEAR OLD MONASTERY HOUSES OVER A 1000 MONKS AND HERE THE NEW MOON FESTIVAL IS THE BIGGEST EVENT OF THE YEAR.

● 93 AT DONGZHULIN MONASTERY, MONKS ENTER THE MAIN PRAYER HALL FOR MORNING MEDITATION, PREPARING LUNCH AND YAK BUTTER TEA.

Cultural Heart and Soul

chapter 3

Cultural Heart and Soul
CHAPTER THREE

My second trip to Kham in the spring of 2009 began in Chengdu, Sichuan, which became my base for the rest of the year. My long-time fixer, Fu Qing, is a native of Sichuan. His company, Kham Trek, arranges and outfits tours for foreigners through Kham and Tibet, not an easy task considering the difficult terrain and even more complicated politics. But Fu is a seasoned mountaineer and an insider in the Tibetan world, having spent many years leading tours there with his Tibetan partner, Jampa. He is the go-to person for the latest on travel conditions and most importantly, for answers to the big question: Is the road open to foreigners past Kangding and Zheduo Pass?

Among those waiting for word on the subject that June was another client of Fu Qing, Dick Grace, an internationally famed California vintner and philanthropist, who has been building orphanages and schools throughout the Tibetan Himalayas. As lovers of all things Tibetan, Dick and I became fast friends while waiting for our permits for access to Tibet. By another stroke of photographer's luck, Dick's current project happened to be the construction of a school at Shechen Monastery in a remote northwest corner of Sichuan, close to the Qinghai border. Once we learned the road was open, I made plans to immediately head to Shechen, knowing that with Dick's introduction we would get a friendly reception.

I was hoping to get an intimate look at life inside a major monastery of 750 monks at its most active season — the festive summer months when the grasslands come alive with celebrations. We were not disappointed. Tashi Tsering, Shechen's chief monk, took me under his wing for the next five days. I knew from previous experience that Tibetans, especially monks at monasteries and during religious ceremonies, were reticent about having their pictures taken and made it nearly impossible to gain access. But with Tashi, I was welcomed at every event, even during prayer and meditation sessions, and I had the run of every temple I visited.

Days at Shechen started early. At 4 a.m., we ambled down a half-mile to the temple kitchen building to start the fires to heat yak butter tea. Two huge cauldrons filled with water were perched atop earthen ovens. (Water boils rapidly in the rarefied air at an altitude of 12,000 ft [3800 m]). Huge balls of yak butter, a bucket of salt and a full bale of tea leaves and twigs were added to the mix, as smoke billowed from the oven firebox and steam filled the air.

Red-robed monks stood above the cauldrons, half-revealed then hidden again by the smoky haze, stirring the soup with huge wooden paddles. I was totally mesmerized by this medieval scene.

By 6:30 a.m., tea for 700 was ready to be served as dawn broke over the valley. My sole source of light is a single open door with a half dozen low-watt bare bulbs for fill, but thanks to digital cameras with high ISOs, I can shoot in available light in what would have been impossible conditions for film. The youngest novice monks sped up and down rows of thirsty monks who had been praying and meditating in the near-freezing temperatures of the monastery's unheated main hall for the past hour, filling bowls with the steaming butter tea and running back to the kitchen for refills. Others pass roasted barley flour, *tsampa*, the staple of the Tibetans' limited diet, which is mixed into the tea for a hearty porridge or rolled into bite-sized balls.

It was all over in half an hour as sated monks headed for the door—some to classes, others to chores. Their next gathering was for noonday prayers and a yak stew lunch, followed by more meditation, prayers and afternoon tea. The rest of their day was spent on preparations and practice for their presentation for the Ling Gesar Festival, which in less than a week would be performed for the public for the first time. Ling Gesar, also known as King Gesar of Ling, is the beloved folk hero who united the country in a series of battles in the 11th century and is believed by Tibetans to be the founder of Tibet. After practice and prayers, without TV or even radio to connect to the outside world, lights go out early.

When visiting a Tibetan monastery, one cannot help but be moved by the spirit of Tibetan monks and their devotion to their brand of Buddhism. It was raining as I packed up my cameras and followed Tashi back to his quarters. He kept up a conversation on his cell phone as we ambled up the mountain, and every few steps he would stop and stoop to pick up earthworms that had surfaced in the rain. Without missing a beat, he would dig a small hole with his bare hands and gently place a worm inside, then cover it with a handful of dirt. His beliefs, which include reincarnation, hold that all living things are precious and equal; to Tashi, that worm might have been a beloved relative or a dear friend in another life.

Any discussion on Tibetan culture would not be complete without a mention of Dege, whose Gengqing Temple, is second only to Lhasa's Jokhan Temple in a ranking of the most important monasteries in Tibet. Gengqing is home to the 18th century Parkhang Scripture Printing House, also known as Dege Auspicious and Wisdom-Gathering House. The over 217,000 hand-engraved woodblocks housed here are used to print Tibetan Buddhist sacred scriptures and prayers, making it the largest repository of Tibetan literature in the world.

I entered the Parkhang through the main entrance, squeezing past hundreds of Tibetan Buddhist devotees doing the *kora*, the ritual clockwise circumambulation around temples, stupas or other sacred sites. The *kora* is part pilgrimage and part meditation and may be performed while spinning prayer wheels, chanting mantras or prostrating oneself. It's a familiar sight in Tibet, and always fascinating to photograph.

Many pictures later I was inside shooting what are actually the last stages of the printing process, as workers washed red ink off 300-year-old woodblocks used the day before. On the second floor under the "No Taking Pictures" sign, I photographed a hundred or so workers laboring—inking blocks and printing thousands of pages per day by hand. No one objected or complained, as I was told that we were the first visitors in over six months. One of the oddities and benefits of traveling in the restricted zone, I was to discover, was that the locals, who hadn't seen a foreign visitor in months and had lost much of the income they make from the tourist trade, were extremely friendly and welcoming. Throughout the remainder of our trip, I was able to shoot without objection, protest or charge.

I soon fell into the rhythm of the inking and rolling, paper to woodblock. The teams of workers intent on printing out pages of scriptures barely noticed me. I made my way to the third floor and headed to the binding room for the final step in the process. Here, bathed in warm morning light, a scholarly group of elders put pages in order and inked them by hand into oblong books for shipment to monasteries all along the Chamagudao route, just as has been done here for three hundred years.

• 103 A young monk runs for a refill of butter tea for the 80 monks at Litang Monastery.

• 104-105 The road at the top of the 16,400 ft (5100 m) Trola Pass, which lies between Dege and Manigango, is covered with snow for most of the year.

• 106-107 The pink prayer flags at the Maiwa Waque Pagoda Park adorn this sacred place.

• 108-109 The hillside above the Segyagu Meditation Center is obscured by thousands of flags, which send prayers to the winds to disperse blessings throughout the land.

• 110-111 Nuns prepare for class in the main hall of Yarchen Gar, the largest community of nuns in the world, where more than 10,000 women of all ages come to study Tibetan Buddhism.

● 112-113 A MONK IN GANDZE PREPARES THE TRADITIONAL FLATBREAD OF CENTRAL TIBET, CALLED *BALEP KORKUN*. IT IS COOKED ON A GRIDDLE AND MADE WITH BARLEY FLOUR, WATER AND BAKING POWDER.

● **114-115** Monks at Gandze Monastery, the most important in Kham, prepare yak butter tea for the 370 monks living there. The black brick tea is mixed with butter and salt.

● **116-117** Young monks are up early to help serve the traditional rice and tea breakfast for the monks at Gandze Monastery.

● **118-119** Lunch times in monasteries are far from somber, as monks of all ages devour a simple meal of yak stew.

● **120-121** A Buddhist nun, who has renounced all worldly things, is anointed in Gandze.

• **122** Wood, which will fuel the stoves and warm the rooms of the monasteries, is a precious commodity on the Tibetan Plateau.

• **122-123** A young monk carries water from a mountain stream back to the Shechen Monastery. The master monk here was once a teacher of the Dalai Lama.

● 124 AND 125 YARCHEN GAR MONASTERY, HOME TO AN ESTIMATED 10,000 TIBETAN NUNS. THEY LIVE ON THIS ISLAND ON THE CHANGQU RIVER IN 3X3 METER BOX HUTS. AT OVER 4,000 METERS, THE WEATHER CAN GET BITTERLY COLD, AND TENTS AND ONLY

126-127 Mt. Kailash is Tibet's most sacred mountain, a pilgrimage site for Indians and Nepalese as well. Buddhists, Hinduis and Bon religion believers all come to do the kora around the mountain distance of 31 mile (50 km).

● **128-129** Monasteries close to Mt. Kailash provide accommodation for pilgrims. Only the most devout will do the arduous 31 mile (50 km) kora, a 3 day hike at over 16,000 ft (4,8 m).

● **130-131** This mother and child have been doing the kora, the clockwise circumambulation of Gung Qing Monastery in Derge.

● 132-133 MONKS AT SHECHEN MONASTERY PREPARE FOR THE ANNUAL REENACTMENT OF THE EPIC STORY OF LING GESAR, THE FATHER OF TIBET. THE LEGEND OF THIS MYTHIC 11TH-CENTURY KING WHO WAGED WAR WITH ENEMIES OF TIBET AND UNIFIED THE COUNTRY THROUGH HIS SUPER-HUMAN CONQUESTS WAS WRITTEN IN 1716 AND IS CONSIDERED THE LONGEST LITERARY WORK IN THE WORLD.

ing Gesar Festival is a time for high spirits and celebration the Shechen monks and the many locals who attend.

aiting in the wings, a monk in warrior costume awaits his cue to battle at the Ling Gesar reenactment, which is performed in July during the grassland festival season.

● **136** There is always time for a butter tea break, even between acts of the Ling Gesar Festival reenactment.

● **137** Since all roles, even female ones, are played by Shechen monks, these "maidens" bringing offerings of kata (ceremonial prayer scarf) and tea to the king are really young boys.

● **138 AND 139** A PROCESSION OF LING GESAR'S WARRIOR GENERALS HEADS INTO BATTLE ADORNED IN ELABORATE HAND-MADE COSTUMES AND HEADDRESSES.

• **140** In addition to dramatizing the Ling Gesar epic, monks of all ages also perform traditional Tibetan dances at the festival.

• **141** Male monks who portray women in the epic wear floral headdresses and jewelry made of coral and silver. In Tibetan culture, jewelry has spiritual, as well as decorative, significance.

• **142-143** Local girls, wearing hair ornaments of amber and coral, are absorbed in the action on the field–a depiction of the legendary horse race won by Ling Gesar, which established him as King of Tibet.

● 144 In a contest of good versus evil, the mighty warrior King Gesar vanquishes his foe, who like bad guys everywhere, is dressed in black.

● 144-145 Ling Gesar takes on another symbol of evil. The enemies portrayed during the festival may be humans or monsters, but in all cases, good conquers bad, and Ling Gesar and his minions triumph.

• 146-147 Halloween-masked monks portray the enemies of Tibet. Evil demons and monsters are depicted as skeletons.

• 148-149 Prayer flags in primary colors symbolizing the five elements offer protection for the newly constructed dormitories at Dege Gonchen.

• 150-151 The Parkhang houses over 200,000 blocks engraved with Tibetan literature, history, medicine and religious writing, making it the cultural heart of Tibet. The printing house is in a traditional temple, which was restored in 1991.

• 152-153 At the Dege Parkhang books are made in the same way as they have been for almost 300 years, from blocks that are hand carved and inked, then printed into long strips, dried and bound into volumes.

• 154-155 Hand-carved wood blocks, which are inked with vermillion ground from the mineral cinnabar, must be cleaned after each use.

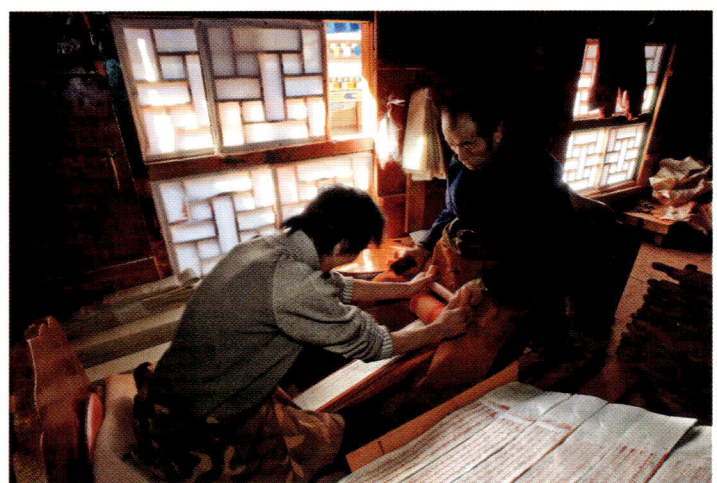

• **156** Printers working in pairs ink and then roll paper over the wood block engraved with text.

• **156-157** Master scholars proofread and assemble the pages by hand into bound books. Efforts are underway to help ensure that these ancient techniques are not lost with modernization.

● 158-159 There are no computerized filing systems or databases to streamline storage and filing at Dege Parkhang; rather each wooden block is assigned its own shelf and accessed via its long handle.

Nomads Land

chapter 4

Nomads Land
Chapter Four

The Tibetan Plateau is arguably the harshest living environment on the planet, but what looks like a barren, treeless landscape is prime grassland for herds of yaks, sheep and goats. Here, often on the highest passes along the Chamagudao, clans of *drokpas* (nomads) spend eight or nine months a year fattening their animals for market, returning to their homes in town for just two or three months during the coldest days of winter. They're easy to spot, usually in groups of five to 15 families, in their unmistakable black yak-hair yurts or government-issue white or blue tents, but they and their lifestyle are fast disappearing as China tries to resettle nomads into permanent housing in towns and villages. Because I've always been fascinated by rugged people who live on the edge under severe conditions, they were at the top of my shot list.

We arrived in nomad country near Serxu, on the Sichuan/Qinghai border far above the tree line at 15,000 ft (4500 m), in the middle of a driving snowstorm—in late May. I photographed yaks silhouetted against a green hillside through a diffusion screen of heavy flakes until the herd disappeared behind a blinding curtain of snow. After that, we headed for a cluster of tents nearby whose chimneys were belching smoke. We were welcomed with lots of *tashi deles* (hellos) and rounds of yak butter tea. Tupten, our host, told us it was the middle of *yartsa gombu* season, a two-month window when all nomads take to their grasslands in search of a strange looking, but highly valued mushroom (*Cordyceps* in English). This parasitic fungus, only found at high altitudes on the Tibetan Plateau, produces the world's most expensive herbal medicine. In Beijing and Shanghai, it commands ¥500,000 per kilo ($76,000 for just over two pounds)—far more than the price of gold.

In winter, the larva of the ghost moth is invaded by a fungus, which then eats the larva from within. In the spring and early summer, the gnarly stem of the mushroom, growing out of what looks like a petrified worm, pops above ground. Its Chinese name, *chong cao*, says it all—"winter worm, summer grass."

Eaten whole, or consumed in capsule or tea form, *yartsa gombu* is believed by the Chinese to cure almost anything, from impotence and Alzheimer's to cancer and SARS (Severe Acute Respiratory Syndrome). In fact, it was the SARS virus epidemic of 2003 that first brought worldwide attention and a sharp spike in price for *yartsa gombu*.

Even at the source, up above 14,000 ft (4500 m) on the Tibetan Plateau, the nomad pickers get the equivalent of $5 to $10 per "worm." With an average harvest of 50 worms per person a day, you have the makings of a gold rush with every man, woman and child out on the grasslands with noses to the ground in search of strange worm-like mushrooms poking up from the earth.

The money nomads make from selling *yartsa gombu* gives them access to what middle-class Han Chinese now take for granted. The main form of transport for the nomads is no longer the sure-footed Tibetan horse, but the motorcycle; waterproof clothing from North Face or Patagonia is just as likely to be worn as yak skin coats and fur hats. Cell phones, even iPhones and iPods, are common, and permanent winter houses in town and good schools for their children are all within reach. *Yartsa gombu* is changing the face of Tibet, making the traditional nomad lifestyle a relic of the past. It's the new currency, replacing tea and horses, along the Chamagudao.

Tupten invited us to join him on a mushroom hunt early the next day, so we spent that first night in nomad's land in his white, government-issue tent, which he said he preferred to the traditional yak-hair style, as it's waterproof and brighter on the inside. Fu and I settled in with Tupten, his wife, Gatseng, daughter Tsering Dolma and son Gompa Dundze. The more bodies the merrier in a Tibetan nomad tent, all the better to keep warm. Unfortunately, the sounds of snoring and feisty mastiff guard dogs barking, as well as my own frequent trips outside into the snow thanks to the diuretic I was taking to combat altitude sickness, made sleep difficult.

The next morning we were up at dawn, or at least Gatseng and I were. In Tibetan nomad cultures, it is the wife who is up first to feed the yak-dung fire to heat the water for the tea and *tsampa*. She then shovels the snow around the perimeter of the tent before heading out to wrangle a dozen *dri* (female yaks) back towards the tent for milking. An hour later, finished with that chore, Gatseng collected more yak dung for the fire before awakening her husband and the rest of our crew for a breakfast of *tsampa* and instant ramen noodles, and of course, butter tea. With full stomachs, we, along with twenty more members of the Tupten clan, jumped on motorcycles and headed for the *yartsa gombu* gathering grounds about an hour's drive away, at 16,000 ft (5000 m).

With handmade picks for digging worms tucked into their belts and empty red ramen bags to hold their macabre treasures stuffed into their pockets, the group literally ran from spot to spot whenever a family member found a specimen. After exchanging a few comments on size and quality, off they'd go again in different directions, heads within inches of the ground. I was right there with them, cameras inches from the ground, trying to take a picture before the nomads were off to the next mushroom-hunting grounds in search of more found money.

At lunchtime, one of the women suggested a more scenic spot up another several hundred meters at the crest of a hill. I groaned as I gathered myself up for another arduous hour's climb. I watched my newfound friends in admiration as they ran up the mountain; Fu and I followed at a quarter of their speed. But later that afternoon, as we made our descent, Fu complained of a major headache and a heavy, pounding heart. He was no better when we reached the motorcycles and headed down another several hundred meters. That evening he had no appetite, ate little, and retired early. The next morning Fu felt even worse. He had awakened from a fitful sleep with a racing heart and was coughing up blood. Suspecting altitude sickness, we knew we needed to head for a lower elevation, so we set out for Yushu, in Qinghai province, a five-hour drive away. This town, with an elevation of about 12,000 ft (3700 m) is noted for the massive earthquake that leveled it in 2010, turning it into a tent city. We found the only doctor in town, who had set up shop in a makeshift shelter when the earthquake destroyed the city's hospital. He confirmed that we were dealing with HAPE (high altitude pulmonary edema), a serious and sometimes fatal altitude sickness. He administered oxygen, but ordered us to descend even lower. By the fourth day, after driving for 16 hours, we had made it to Xining, where Fu got to a proper hospital. But even here, at just over 7000 ft (2100 m) the doctors felt the elevation was too high, so they instructed Fu to head home as soon as possible—but via train, not air, as he was still dangerously sick. We put Fu on soft-sleeper train bound for Chengdu and some much needed rest and relaxation. Back home, he recuperated quickly.

Fixers like Fu are the unsung heroes of journalism. They act as guide, producer, coordinator, researcher, interpreter, secretary, accountant, restaurant critic, bag handler, and sometimes driver—and Fu is one of the best. He is also a knowledgeable and amiable travel companion. Once he was out of danger, I couldn't help noting the irony in the fact that despite *yartsa gombu*'s reputation for curing hundreds of maladies, HAPE is not on the list.

• 163 A nomad grandmother multi-tasks, making time for a hug and a kiss while churning yak butter. She and her family of seven will spend the summer here, 12 miles (20 km) from their home near Bame.

• 166-167 Along Route 318, the southern route of the Chamagudao, the Zar Gamala Pass is the highest vertical climb in Tibet from 5,570 ft (1,700 m) to 15,282 ft (4,658 m). Adding further to the thrills of traversing it are 180 switchbacks.

• 168-169 Yaks are indispensible to the Tibetan nomads, providing warmth and sustenance. Ideally adapted to the high altitudes and cold temperatures of the Tibetan Plateau, yaks are perfect pack animals, sturdy and sure-footed.

• **170 AND 170-171** WOMEN AND YOUNGSTERS TAKE CARE OF MOST OF THE DOMESTIC CHORES, WHICH INCLUDE SHEEP SHEARING. SHEEP ARE ALMOST AS USEFUL TO THE TIBETANS AS YAK, PROVIDING WOOL, MEAT, HIDES AND MILK.

• 172-173 Nomad families spend the summer months living together in yak-hair tents, grazing their animals and searching for the valuable *yartsa gombu* (cordyceps) caterpillar fungus.

• 174-175 An early snowstorm veils a herd of yaks grazing along the Yalong River.

• **176** A nomad cowboy, as sturdy and rugged as his mount, trains his horse for the summer racing season.

• **176-177** Traditional black yak-hair tents have sheltered nomad families for centuries from the harsh and unpredictable weather of the Tibetan Plateau.

● **178-179** A YOUNG MOTHER STARTS THE COOKING FIRE FOR HER FAMILY OF SEVEN, WHILE HER SON WATCHES AND LEARNS. THREE GENERATIONS OF THIS *DROPKA* (NOMAD) FAMILY LIVE TOGETHER IN THEIR TENT.

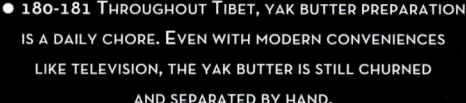

• 180-181 Throughout Tibet, yak butter preparation is a daily chore. Even with modern conveniences like television, the yak butter is still churned and separated by hand.

• 182-183 Silhouetted against an early morning sunrise, a nomad encampment is situated along Route 109, near the sacred Namtso Lake.

• 184-185 The white canvas tents provided by the Chinese government are increasingly preferred to the traditional black yak-hair tents by today's nomads, like this family camped near Hei Tu Shan Pass in prime cordyceps-gathering territory.

• 186-187 Tibetans call these multi-colored flags "wind horses." They are hung to protect travelers crossing through the often-treacherous mountain passes.

● 188-189 AND 191 THE *DRI* (FEMALE YAKS) STILL NEED MILKING, DESPITE AN EARLY SNOW, AND THE JOB FALLS TO THE WOMAN OF THE TENT.

● 193 Tibetans are never without their tea and drink an average of 40 cups a day. Ten-year-old Tsering Dolna, slathered in lotion to protect against the intense sun, sips her butter tea, adding precious calories to her diet.

● **194** Keen eyesight and patience are required to spot the well-camouflaged *yartsa gombu*, which protrudes only a half-inch above the ground. Formed when a fungus invades the body of a caterpillar, it is said to have near-miraculous medicinal powers and holds the promise of riches for Tibetan nomads.

● **194-195** Replacing herding as a livelihood for nomads, harvesting *yartsa gombu* involves the entire family. Using handmade spades and trowels, the caterpillar fungus is hacked out of the ground.

- **196** Motorcycles, purchased with the profits from *yartsa gombu* sales, are replacing horses for families like the Tuptens, who are camped near Hei Tu Shan Pass.

- **196-197** A motorcycle built for two does double duty for these nomads on the trail of the *yartsa gombu*, which translated literally means "winter worm, summer grass."

- **198-199** Nomads gather in Serxu, the world's highest town at 13,600 ft (4150 m) to clean and display their wares, their trusty Tibetan ponies unaware that they are fast becoming obsolete.

● **200** Like ladies at an old fashioned quilting bee, workers begin the task of cleaning the mushrooms brought in by nomad traders to Yushu, in Qinghai province.

● **200-201** Muslim Uighurs control the mushroom trade, employing women like these in their millinery finery, to sort, clean and dry the *yartsa gombu* in Xining, capital of Qinghai.

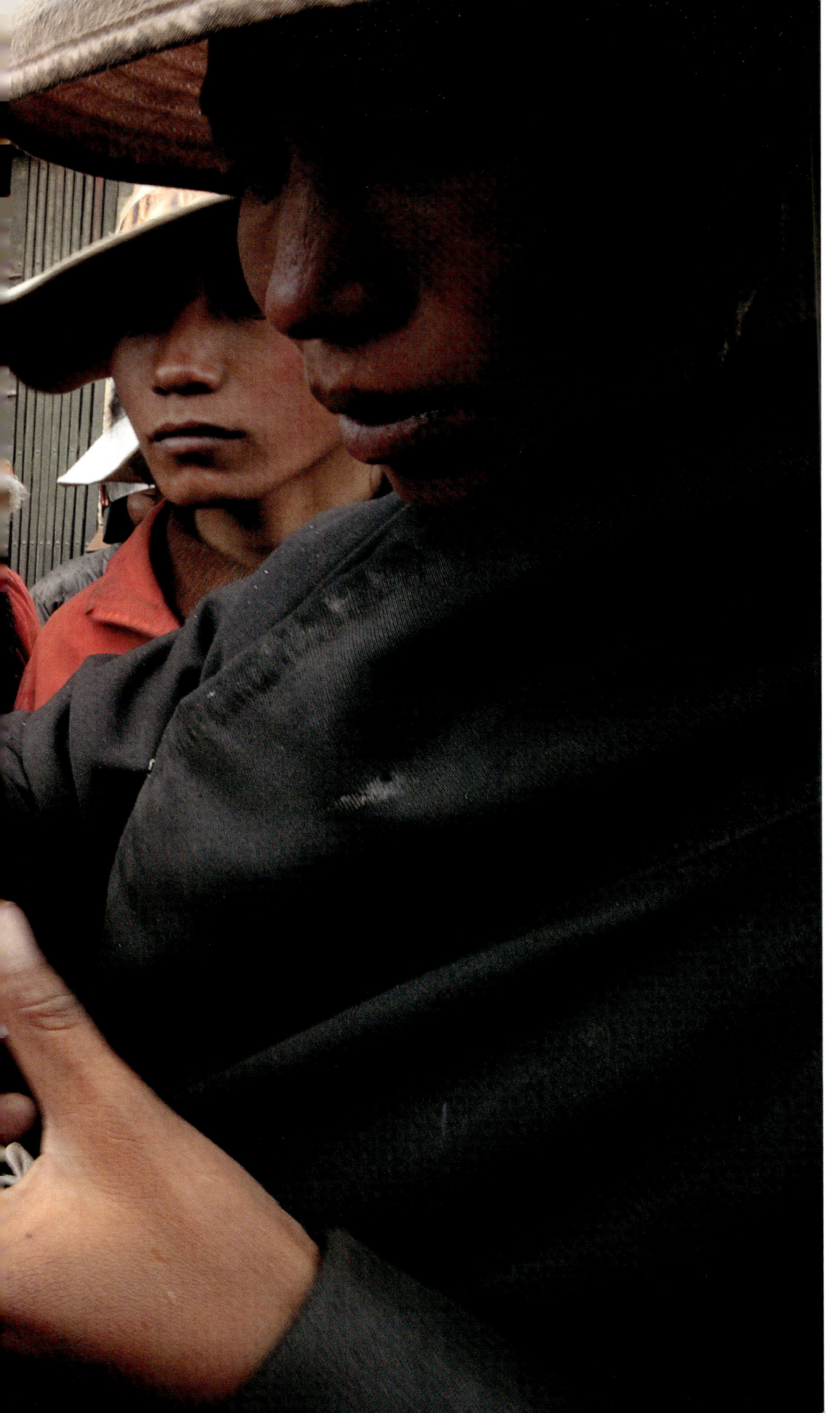

● 202-203 Fresh from foraging for *yartsa gombu* on the grasslands, this nomad shows some prime specimens to traders.

● 204-205 A hundred years ago, Tibetan horses would have been tied up in front of these storefronts in Serxu, but today, the motorcycle is the nomad's preferred means of transport.

On the Road to Lhasa and the Top of the World

chapter 5

On the Road to Lhasa and the Top of the World
Chapter Five

Our next and final challenge was getting into the Tibet Autonomous Region (TAR), which at any time is a complicated procedure requiring several levels of permits from the Public Security Bureau (PSB) in Lhasa on down to those from the local towns and villages. Any guidebook will tell you that when applying for a China visa, never list Tibet or any city in Tibet under the "places to be visited section" or your visa will be denied. And under "occupation" never state *photographer*. If you do, your visa will be automatically rejected, and you will be forced to apply for a journalist visa, which may or may not be approved, depending on what might be happening politically in China at the time, as well as on the unpredictable level of paranoia of the Chinese government.

In areas as sensitive as Tibet, permits for photographers who are considered to be journalists are just not allowed, period. So I traveled as a tourist in a group of three—Fu Qing, now fully recovered from HAPE, our driver Huka and me. And on our list of places to go were the rest of the northern Chamagudao, Route 317, as well as the entire southern route, 318. Thanks to Fu's connections in Lhasa we got all that we asked for.

One of the constants of travel on the road to Lhasa is the procession of pilgrims along the route. I will never forget the first time I encountered a pilgrim performing the Tibetan Buddhist act of prostration known as *chak tsal*; it was on the road to Labrang Monastery in Gansu Province. I jumped out of the car with camera in hand and got down on my stomach to shoot just as he laid out flat in front of me, face to the ground. I followed his every movement—a couple of steps, palms together, *click*; another step, hands to the heart, *click*; hands to face, *click* and hands overhead, *click*. Then he was back down to his knees and flat out on his stomach again, *click*. Forehead to the ground, *click*. After five or six repetitions of this exercise, I was exhausted in the thin air and sat by the side of the road for a rest, but the pilgrim kept right on going up the hill. During the entire time I was shooting he never acknowledged my presence, praying and prostrating as if I were not even there. I got up and followed to ask him a few questions. He answered without stopping. His name was Champa and he was en route to Labrang. He had been on the road for two months, and hoped to make it to the great monastery in time for Losar, the Tibetan New Year. From there he planned to continue on to Lhasa, a 1242 mi (2000 km) journey that he hoped to complete in another 200 days.

I thanked him for his time and forbearance at my disturbance of his prayer and drove on another three hours to Xiahe. Several days later, I ran into Champa again as he was prostrating his way clockwise around Labrang following the *kora* for a few days or weeks before continuing on to his ultimate goal, the Jokhan Temple in Lhasa, which is the lifelong dream of every Tibetan. I was humbled by this man's spirit, incredible determination and endurance, and unshakeable faith. I was to meet many more men like Champa in the next six weeks along the road to Lhasa. In fact, the closer we got to Lhasa, the more pilgrims we met, building in numbers to the Potala Palace itself.

But one important subject continued to evade me—where were all the horses? Back in the Ming Dynasty heyday of the Chamagudao, as many as 25,000 horses a year were traded for thousands of pounds of tea. But today, horses and donkeys are rarely used, save for in the poorest of villages. For the farmer, horse-drawn plows have been replaced by tractors; for the nomads, herding work once done by horses on the grasslands is now handled by motorcycles, affordable to all thanks to the *yartsa gombu* mushroom. And caravans, which were once the only means of long-distance transportation of tea and other commodities, have been replaced by trucks. The few horses we did see were idle, grazing peacefully in pastures.

But during the short summer month of August that all changes, as horses once again serve a purpose: racing at the summer festivals that were once held annually all across Kham and Tibet. Now they're strictly limited in size, scale and frequency, often cancelled by the government if there is a rise in the number of Tibetan protests or demonstrations. We were lucky in 2009 to catch the biggest horse festival, in Nakchu. Having been cancelled the year before, during the Olympics, the excitement among the Tibetan horsemen was palpable.

The Nakchu festival draws as many as 10,000 people, who set up tents on the race track grounds south of town. Nomad cowboys on horseback arrive from every direction, charging in at a full gallop for the last 650 ft (200 m) up to the edge of the festival grounds in groups of two, four, and ten or more. They dismount with a swaggering flourish, knowing all eyes are on them. Everyone wears the best of traditional costumes: women in the long robes called *chuba*, and draped in layers of gold and turquoise jewelry; men in Stetson hats, knee-high boots and long-sleeved tunics. Assorted contests and shows of prowess are presented, from archery to tug of war. But the main attraction is horse racing.

The racecourse here is said to be the highest in the world, and the small, sturdy horses that take part in the friendly competitions are uniquely suited to the altitude. But for added energy in the races, I'm told that they get an extra boost, in the form of soaked tea leaves.

Despite the show of equestrian skills put on the by nomad riders for the races, which are the highlight of the day, the focus is not on the adults but on their kids and teenagers, the lighter the better. They, not the adult cowboys, are the jockeys. How odd, I thought, that my final opportunity to shoot the once feared Tibetan warhorse of the Chinese Emperor's armies would turn out to be with me in the stands, watching the legendary horses racing around a track, ridden by children.

● **209** Devout pilgrims proceed at a snail's pace performing the *chak tsal*, the Tibetan name for ritual prostration. Their journey from Qinghai will take six months, along the northern branch of the Tea Horse Road to the sacred city of Lhasa.

● **211** Color is everywhere in Tibet, from prayer flags to the turquoise and coral ornaments and costumes of both men and women.

● **212-213** A lone horse grazes on land near the mountain pass west of the nomad town of Manigango, where the Tea Horse Road split into its northern and western branches.

214-215 A *MANI* PRAYER STONE SITS ON THE SHORE OF LHAMO LATSO, A LAKE SACRED TO TIBETANS, AT THE FOOT OF THE TROLA MOUNTAIN RANGE.

● **216-217** Summer means time for the annual bath for these young monks soaking in the Rombatsa Hot Springs. Due to the harsh climate, most Tibetans bathe only once or twice a year.

• 218-219 Once a common sight, it is now rare to see herds of Tibetan horses on the grasslands of the plateau.

• **220-221** There are still those who transport their goods the old fashioned way, like this woman toting brick tea from the market in Rombatsa.

• 222 AND 222-223 A WOMAN ADDS HER PRAYERS TO THE GROWING MOUNTAIN OF MORE THAN A BILLION *MANI* STONES AT GYANAMANI TEMPLE, IN YUSHU, AN AREA ROCKED BY EARTHQUAKES IN 2010. THIS COLLECTION OF HAND-CARVED STONES WITH BUDDHIST SUTRAS AND SYMBOLS IS THE LARGEST IN THE WORLD.

• 224-225 These men show that one needn't be standing to receive the benefits and good karma of a clockwise turn of a prayer wheel.

• **226-227** Prayer flags inscribed with Buddhist *sutra* (prayers) frame Namtso Lake in primary colors, representing the five basic elements.

• **228-229** Along the the Yarlung Tsangpo River, the longest river in Tibet and source of the Brahmaputra in India.

• **230-231** Xiayigou Earth Forest is known as Tibet's Grand Canyon. Along the Xiangquan (Elephant Spring) River, odd shaped rock forms are carved out by water and wind erosion.

• **232-233** With trucks and motorcycles taking over the jobs of herding and transport, Tibetan cowboys like these in Chiusang, an hour north of Lhasa, find work as guides for tourist trekkers.

• **234-235** Tibetan cowboys in their long coats called *chubas* and Stetson hats wait their turn to show off their horsemanship.

• 236-237 AND 237 YOUNG WOMEN IN TYPICALLY COLORFUL TIBETAN COSTUMES PRIMP BEFORE THEIR UPCOMING TRADITIONAL DANCE PERFORMANCE AT THE FESTIVAL.

• 238 A YOUNG GIRL'S FINERY COMES OUT FOR THE FESTIVAL, FROM RED FOX FUR HAT TO LAYERS OF ORNATE JEWELRY.

• 239 A COWBOY'S ONE WARDROBE ESSENTIAL IS HIS WESTERN-STYLE FELT HAT.

• **240-241** Every part of a Tibetan's traditional costume, from colorful robes to fur hats to necklaces and earrings, carry centuries of meaning and symbolism. Turquoise, coral and amber are believed to have healing and protective powers.

• **242-243** Not to be outdone by the ladies, these men wear heirloom costumes made with leopard and tiger skins and red fox fur hats.

• **244-245** They're off for the main event: Boy jockeys on surefooted mounts tear away from the starting line at breakneck speed.

Elusive Shangri-La

chapter 6

Elusive Shangri-La
CHAPTER SIX

One of the most brilliant marketing moves in China's brief modern history is the 2001 renaming of the town of Zhongdian in northern Yunnan to its present designation—Shangri-La—after the fictional mountain paradise imagined by novelist James Hilton in his novel, *Lost Horizon*. After all, the town *is* high up on the Tibetan Plateau, and if you come from the north, you do have to cross several mountain ranges to get there. The climate is rather ideal, and the mostly Tibetan inhabitants are friendly. Zhongdian also has the requisite monastery, located in a setting worthy of *Lost Horizon*'s movie version.

Written in 1933, the book is believed to have been inspired by the work of the legendary *National Geographic* explorer, Joseph Rock, who once lived nearby in the town of Lijiang. Between 1922 and 1935, Rock wrote and photographed ten articles on the region for the magazine. He was also an old friend of mine, of sorts, since it was Rock, or at least his work, that introduced me to the Tibetan world. In preparation for my *National Geographic* story on him ("Our Man in China," January 1997), I immersed myself in his writing and photography about Tibet, and on my first trip to Zhongdian/Shangri-La in 1997, I photographed the same monastery, little changed since Rock described it more than 80 years before.

Rock was a formidable linguist who spoke ten languages, including Tibetan, as well as seven aboriginal dialects of Chinese. He traveled on horseback along the Chamagudao, with as many as 200 men and muleteers. His entourage included a cook, servants and even armed soldiers to keep bandits at bay. Dressed in a white shirt, jacket and tie, the Austrian-born Rock dined on Viennese cuisine cooked by a Chinese chef he trained himself. His meals were served on fine china and on a table, complete with linen tablecloth and silver cutlery. He even bathed daily in a portable bathtub, bought from the expedition outfitter Abercrombie and Fitch, while listening to Italian opera played on a battery-operated phonograph. I admired the man's style and marveled at his generous *National Geographic* expense account.

It was a fitting tribute, then, to be back following in the footsteps of Rock. I was on my own search for Shangri-La in the county now named Shangri-La, which was inspired by *Lost Horizon*, which was in turn, inspired by Rock. The day I reached Zhongdian this time around, I was deep into *Lost Horizon* and like the book's protagonist, had arrived by plane, but instead of crashing into a snow bank as Conrad did, I landed at Shangri-La's brand-spanking new airport, built to accommodate the tourists who now flock to this remote town.

After shooting Zhongdian/Shangri-La, trying to evoke the sense of an earthly paradise through its most noteworthy sights—Sumzanling Monastery, Mekong River gorge, and Kawagebo Snow Mountain (often depicted on covers of *Lost Horizon*)—I was eager to turn our attention to Lhasa. Lhasa, I thought, was going to be the culmination of what I'd been looking for—an almost mythic city with its looming Potala Palace, once home to the Dalai Lama, the sacred Jokhan Temple and the Barkor, part marketplace, part sacred site for prayerful pilgrims performing the *kora*. After two years of working on this story, our arrival there, which should have been a crowning moment of celebration, instead turned out to be something of a letdown.

One of my golden rules of travel is to avoid expecting too much or risk disappointment. In the case of Lhasa, though, I broke my own rule and arrived with the baggage of too many expectations for this holiest of Tibetan cities. It would have been hard not to have high hopes for what I would find in here. No place could have lived up to them, even if modernity and China hadn't encroached. As we finally arrived in Lhasa, I couldn't shake the feeling that I was twenty years too late.

Up until the past century, Lhasa was a bustling market city at the crossroads of the Tea-Horse trade, and was also a magnet for Buddhists from all over the world. The influx of the Chinese has swept away much of what made Lhasa so distinct. The Lhasa of today is a mostly modern Chinese city, with only a few fine examples of Tibetan architecture and traditions remaining. Even the Potala Palace had been turned into a museum piece on display for tourists.

I needed to capture a vision of the Lhasa as it might have seemed to a trader arriving along the ancient Chamagudao, without the tour groups and traffic and nondescript buildings of a 21st century city. A photograph taken in 1981 by my friend and fellow *National Geographic* photographer, the late, great Galen Rowell became my inspiration. In this picture, one of the most iconic photographs ever taken in Tibet and Galen's most memorable image, the Potala Palace, epitomizing all the mystery and majesty of ancient Tibet, is literally the pot of gold sitting at the end of a perfect rainbow.

To shoot this monument, Galen, well known for his athletic prowess, literally ran a mile chasing a rainbow, no small feat at Lhasa's altitude of 11,450 ft (3700 m). He had spotted the

rainbow in the early evening sky behind the Potala Palace, the most sacred symbol of
Panting in the thin mountain air, he ran to find just the right angle that would place th
bow's end precisely above the top of the Palace. (Sadly, Galen and his wife Barbara pe
in an airplane accident en route to their home in Bishop, California in 2002.)

I stood in front of the towering Potala, which dominates the city and appears to be
the 700 ft (213 m) hill on which it sits, with the vision of Galen's rainbow picture in my
As I tried to figure out the vantage from which he had shot it, I soon realized that it cou
have been from where I was, on the front side, as it would have been impossible to isola
temple from the modern buildings of the surrounding city.

Following this hunch, we drove north around the backside of the Palace, in the direc
a rim of mountains that were opposite an extensive marsh at least a mile away. There w
a building in sight. In the middle of the marsh there was a lake, and in the middle of th
I saw my picture—isolated in the water was a perfect reflection of the Palace surroun
mountains, as if floating on air. This was a view any traveler coming from the north, eve
years ago, might have seen as he entered Lhasa. And there it was, hiding in plain sig
vision of paradise, Shangri-La.

● 250-251 LHASA'S POTALA PALACE, THE MONASTERY THAT WAS HOME TO THE DALI LAMA, IS AMONG THE MOST ICONIC I
OF TIBET. THE PALACE SEEMS TO FLOAT AMONG THE MOUNTAINS, HOVERING ABOVE THE MARSH IN THE FOREGROUND.

● 252-253 KAWAGEBO, THE HIGHEST PEAK IN YUNNAN, LORDS OVER THE MIST-SHROUDED MEILI SNOW MOUNTAINS AROU

• **256 AND 256-257** BENZILAN VILLAGE LIES ALONG THE BANKS OF THE YANGTZE RIVER. NOT FAR FROM HERE IS THE FIRST MAJOR BEND IN THE YANGTZE, WHERE IT MAKES AN ALMOST 180-DEGREE TURN TO THE NORTHEAST.

• **258-259** ROUTE 318 WEAVES THROUGH THE HEART OF SHANGRI-LA COUNTY, PAST FERTILE VALLEYS THAT ARE HOME TO MANY MINORITY PEOPLES WHOSE WAYS HAVE CHANGED LITTLE OVER TIME.

• **260-261** SUMZANLING MONASTERY IN TODAY'S SHANGRI-LA (FORMERLY ZHONGDIAN): IN WORDS THAT COULD DESCRIBE IT TODAY, JAMES HILTON WROTE, "[THE VALLEY WAS] SURVEYED, RATHER THAN DOMINATED BY THE LAMASERY … A DELIGHTFULLY FAVORED PLACE."

● 262-263 A CRAFTSMAN POLISHES THE NOSE OF A GIGANTIC COPPER BUDDHA AT A MONASTERY WORKSHOP IN SHANGRI-LA.

• 264-265 Yi women, known for their colorful and distinctive costumes, prepare a meal in their village near Shaxi. They are among the 40 minorities whose cultures were linked by the Tea Horse Road.

• 266-267 Burning juniper branches as an incense offering to the gods is practiced at Samye Monastery. Three big incense burners between the prayer poles keep the courtyard filled with smoke.

• 268-269 Viewed from the city of Lhasa, with its telephone lines, electric lights and traffic, the Potala Palace is brought back into the focus of modern Chinese life.

Authors

Photographer MICHAEL YAMASHITA has worked for the *National Geographic* magazine for over 35 years, covering wide-ranging topics throughout six continents. His long career has seen him traipse through war zones, deserts and mountains, from the Great Wall of China to Taliban-controlled Afghanistan. Following his graduation from Wesleyan University, he moved to Japan on a self-described "roots trip" and there discovered his passion for photography and travel. He became intrigued by the epic voyages of great explorers, producing magazine features and books on Marco Polo, Basho - Japan's famed haiku poet, the Chinese 15th-century explorer Zheng He and his most recent, *A Silk Road Journey*. In addition to his work for *National Geographic* magazine, he has photographed for many other American and international publications and clients.

A frequent keynote speaker, Yamashita has participated in Ted Talks and has spoken at a variety of photo events around the world. His work has been exhibited at many diverse venues. Known for his engaging teaching style, he has conducted photo workshops and is often called upon to judge international photo competitions. In addition to his still photography, Yamashita has produced two award-winning feature length documentary films, based on his work retracing the journeys of Marco Polo and Zheng He.

ELIZABETH BIBB is a writer and editor who works in both magazine and book publishing. A frequent contributor to national magazines and newspapers, including *Cosmopolitan*, *Seventeen*, *YM*, *New York*, the *Los Angeles Times* and the *Dallas Times Herald*.

The author of three books, *In the Japanese Garden*, *Womb for Rent* and *New York: Flying High*, Bibb is active in play and screenwriting workshops in New York. She is a founding member of the New Jersey Screenwriters Group and has served as dramaturge for the T. Schreiber Studio in New York. Her plays, *Double Dutch* and *Rebecca and Daniel* were performed there in staged readings.

Bibb holds a Master's degree from Columbia University's Graduate School of Journalism and is a frequent collaborator with her husband, *National Geographic* photographer Michael Yamashita, on travel books and articles.

Bibliography

Asiapac Editorial. *Origins of Chinese Tea and Wine*. Singapore: Asiapac Book, 2006.
Booz, R. Patrick. *Yunnan*. Chicago: Passport Books, 1997.
Bowers Museum of Cultural Art. *Tibet: Treasures From the Roof of the World*. Santa Ana, CA: Bowers Museum of Cultural Art, 2003.
Chan, Victor. *Tibet Handbook A Pilgrimage Guide*. Chico, California: Moon Publications, 1994.
Damien Harper, et. al. *China*. Oakland: Lonely Planet, 2005.
Damien Harper, et. al. *China's Southwest*. Oakland: Lonely Planet, 2007.
Dorje, Gyurme. *Tibet*. Bath: Footprint, 2004.
Edwards, Mike. "Our Man in China: Joseph Rock." *National Geographic*, January 1997: 62-81.
Fuchs, Jeff. *The Ancient Tea Horse Road*. Toronto: Penquin Group, 2008.
Heiss, Mary Lou Heiss and Robert J. *The Story of Tea: A Cultural History and Drinking Guide*. Berkeley, CA: Ten Speed Press, 2007.
Hilton, James. *Lost Horizon*. New York, NY: William Morrow & Company, Inc., 1933.
Hoagland, Ed. "Mystic Waters: Jiuzhaigou." *National Geographic*, March 2009: 82-97.
Jenkins, Mark. "The Forgotten Road." *National Geographic*, May 2010: 94-119.
Macfarlane, Alan and Iris. *Green Gold: The Empire of Tea*. London: Ebury Press/Random House, 2004.
Man, Wong How. *From ManChuria To Tibet*. W.W.Norton & Company, 1998.
Moxham, Roy. *Tea: Addiction, Exploitation and Empire*. London: Robinson, 2004.
Nangsa, Lainchung. *Ancient Sichuan-Tibet Tea-Horse Road*. Beijing: Foreign Languages Press, 2007.
Nomachi, Kazuyoshi. *A Photographer's Pilgrimage: 30 years of great reportage*. Vercelli: White Star Publishers, 2005.
Ricard, Matthieu; Follmi, Olivia and Daniel. *Buddhist Himalayas*. New York City, NY: Harry N.Abrams Inc., 2002.
Yun, Sian Yan. *Searching for The Ancient Tea Horse Road*. Taipei: Shu-Jen Chang, 2008.

Acknowledgements:

I would like to thank my publisher, White Star, for this, our fourth collaboration. Thanks to Marcello Bertinetti, Valeria Manferto de Fabianis, Laura Accomazzo, Francesca Piscitello and Paola Piacco.

Thanks to my colleagues at National Geograpic Magazine who have been sending me to Tibetan territory over a period of fifteen years, for stories on Joseph Rock, Marco Polo, Jiuzhaigou National Park, Chamagudao (Tea Horse Road) and Yartsa Gombu: Editors Bill Allen and Chris Johns; Art Director Bill Marr; Directors of Photography Kent Kobersteen, David Griffin and Kurt Mutchler; Picture Editors Susan Welchman, Elizabeth Krist and Sarah Leen and writers Mike Edwards, Mark Jenkins, Mike Finkel and Ted Hoagland.

Thanks also go to my camera sponsors Satoshi Hatano and Synthia Lau at Sony China; to my traveling companions, friends and information resources: Dick Grace, Scott Harrison, Patrick Dowdey, Paddy Booz, Alan and Han Han Yamashita, Ben Lo, Victor Cha, Matthew Hu, Jia Liming, Yungshih Lee, Kazuyoshi Nomachi, Lin Jia Shiui (Jiuzhaigou Park), Chen Shugian (Yaan Tea Association), Eufung Hwang and How Man Wong (CERS). Thanks to Michael Shatzkin and George Steinmetz for their publishing advice. Thanks to my fixers Fu Qing, Michael Deng, Ling Yi Chen and her dad, tea expert Ming Lo Chen; to my drivers Huka and He and to my friends and guides in Tibet: Baima Dorji (of Songstam Lodges), Nyima Wandul, Penkyla at Shechen Monastery, Tashi at Yabshi Phankhang and Yang Kyi Tsering.

Thanks to my wife and editor, Elizabeth Bibb, who wrote the historical introduction and captions and also edits my life, and to Julie Qualman, my office manager for sixteen years who helped put it all together.

And finally, to all the subjects of my photographs–the people of Tibet who allowed me to intrude into their homes, tents and monasteries and to share their meals and lives with a smile–a big thank you for not saying no and for taking the time to teach me about all things Tibetan.

ALL PHOTOGRAPHS ARE BY MICHAEL YAMASHITA EXCEPT THE FOLLOWING:

pages 12-13, 272: Fu Qing - pages 18-19: Martin Gamache/National Geographic Stock.

• **272** MICHAEL YAMASHITA AT THE DEGE PARKHANG PRINTING HOUSE.

COVER: LHASA'S POTALA PALACE, THE MONASTERY THAT WAS HOME TO THE DALI LAMA, IS AMONG THE MOST ICONIC IMAGES OF TIBET.
BACKCOVER: WOMEN HARVESTING TEA ON A PLANTATION IN YA'AN, IN THE PROVINCE OF SICHUAN.
BACK FLAP: MICHAEL YAMASHITA PHOTOGRAPHED BY HIS FRIEND AND COLLEAGUE FU QING.

WHITE STAR PUBLISHERS

WS White Star Publishers® is a registered trademark
property of White Star s.r.l.

© 2012, 2019 White Star s.r.l.
Piazzale Luigi Cadorna, 6 - 20123 Milan, Italy
www.whitestar.it

All photographs © Michael Yamashita

Editing: Sarah M K Mastrian

All rights reserved. No part of this publication may be reproduced, stored in a retrieval system
or transmitted in any form or by any means, electronic, mechanical, photocopying, recording or
otherwise, without written permission from the publisher.

ISBN 978-88-544-1560-7
1 2 3 4 5 6   23 22 21 20 19

Printed in Italy by Rotolito S.p.A. - Seggiano di Pioltello (Milan)